THE R FACTOR®

HOW TO MAXIMIZE THE ONE THING YOU CAN CONTROL

HEATHER VERITY

ISBN: 979-8-9944831-0-7 Paperback
ISBN: 979-8-9944831-1-4 Hardcover
ISBN: 979-8-9944831-2-1 eBook

Scriptor PUBLISHING GROUP

ScriptorPublishingGroup.com

To John, my husband and love of 10,000 lifetimes – without your unconditional love and support, none of this would be possible.

My parents, Tammy and David, and my brothers, Scott and David, who taught me trust and loyalty.

To Derek for introducing me to TK and encouraging that very first conversation. Your faith, belief and dedication from Day 1 will never be forgotten.

The Focus 3 Team who inspire me to all things Elite. Your success, happiness and well-being are the compass that guides my every decision.

To Jody, Rochelle, Frank and Cami for being my "acquisition Angels" and my fierce guardians of all things Focus 3. Your counsel and guidance could not be more valued and appreciated.

To Cory, my deepest appreciation for you having early eyes on the book and "gently" encouraging what the cover should be.

To The friends and family of Bill W. (and you know who you are) Thank you for always providing a safe place to land for our family. Your warmth and generosity will forever be a part of my life.

Welcome to the Journey

Table of Contents

"Our deepest fear is not that we are inadequate. Our deepest fear is that we are powerful beyond measure. It is our light, not our darkness that most frightens us. We ask ourselves, 'Who am I to be brilliant, gorgeous, talented, fabulous?' Actually, who are you not to be? You are a child of God. Your playing small does not serve the world. There is nothing enlightened about shrinking so that other people won't feel insecure around you. We are all meant to shine, as children do. We were born to make manifest the glory of God that is within us. It's not just in some of us; it's in everyone. And as we let our own light shine, we unconsciously give other people permission to do the same. As we are liberated from our own fear, our presence automatically liberates others."

– Marianne Williamson,
A Return to Love: Reflections on the Principles of "A Course in Miracles"

PREFACE

The first section of this book has a special place in its history. Long before I ever sat down to write these pages, the founder of *The R Factor*®, Tim Kight, began shaping a manuscript of his own. It was meant to be the opening to a larger work he planned to complete. Sadly, life moved in other directions, and that book never found its way to the finish line. Even so, his early pages carried a clear intention. They were rooted in his commitment to teach people how to respond with purpose and ownership, no matter the situation.

I chose to include Tim's original writing at the front of this book as a way to honor him. His words created the foundation for everything that came after. They laid out the concepts that have guided teams, families and leaders for years. His voice deserves to be heard here, exactly where he first hoped it would belong.

What follows is his untouched text. It offers a glimpse into his early vision and sets the stage for the journey you and I will take through the rest of this book.

From the Pen of Tim Kight

One of the most powerful attributes you have as a human being is the ability to choose how you respond to the events and situations you experience. The power to choose means you have the capacity to pursue and achieve goals. You have the ability to solve problems and overcome obstacles. You can adapt to changing circumstances and environments. You can impact the lives of other people in a positive way. You can grow and get better all because you have the power of choice.

The freedom to choose is a gift, and with that gift comes the responsibility and opportunity to pursue the best version of you. Not you compared to someone else, but you compared to who you were yesterday. The pathway to the best version of you is simple, but most certainly not easy: Be better today than you were yesterday and be better tomorrow than you are today. Wherever you are in life, you can make the choice to improve who you are and what you are capable of doing.

Choice is powerful, but it's not unlimited. Despite the pretentious claims and extravagant promises of many self-help books, there are limits and constraints to what you can achieve. Having said that, the human capacity to choose and respond is far deeper than most people realize. Sadly, there are many who fall painfully short of maximizing their potential. The reality is that people can accomplish significantly more than they think and therein lies the challenge: the biggest constraint to human achievement is behavior.

Your behavior – how you think, make decisions, and take action – is the one thing in your life that you can evaluate, change, and improve. It's unfortunate that so many people simply quit trying. When it gets difficult or challenging, they give up and give in. They accept mediocrity. They hold on to limiting beliefs. They underestimate what they are capable of doing and achieving. They get stuck and settle for something less than the best version of themselves. Pursuing the best version of you requires continuously improving your mindset and behavior.

Your life is a journey, a great adventure. Like any great adventure, it has twists and turns, ups and downs, easy times and hard times. There are paths to follow, bridges to cross, and mountains to climb. There are mysteries to be solved, dragons to be slain, and treasure to be found. Along the way you will encounter people who are on their own journey. Some of those people will help you, and others will hurt you. Some will encourage you, others will discourage you. Some will collaborate with you, others will undermine you.

Success on the journey is more than just how you perform as an individual. It's also about how you connect and contribute to the people around you. Whether with your family at home or colleagues at your job, your ability to engage others and work together toward a result is a critical skill. Success, as it turns out, is a team sport. You need other people, and other people need you.

Throughout your life journey you have made choices about what paths to follow. It is those choices that have brought you to where you are today, and the choices you make going forward are what will determine your future. The purpose of this book is to awaken you to the power of choice in your life. You'll learn the foundational behavior skills necessary to navigate situations and produce better results, both personally and professionally. It's not about abstract theories, hyped-up motivational quotes, or quick fixes. In the pages that follow, you will discover practical, real-world tools for how to maximize the one thing you control: *How you choose to respond.*

That's why it's called *The R Factor*®.

My journey began in 1972. I was a sophomore at UCLA on a track scholarship running the 440 yard hurdles. Back then, the track team shared the athletic facilities with the basketball team at Pauley Pavilion. Frequently, I would slip into one of the stadium seats after track practice and watch the legendary John Wooden coach his team. Wooden led 8 UCLA men's basketball teams to national championships, and by the time I graduated, they won two more. Ten national championships! A record that was unfathomable during that era and remains unbeaten to this day.

There was something remarkable about the future Hall-of-Famer's demeanor and coaching method. He was intensely competitive, but without anger – a combination I'd never seen before in a coach. Wooden saw the whole picture, while at the same time was laser focused on technique. I began to wonder, "How is it that a single man can be so effective at leading a team, not just to success, but to greatness?"

During my career at UCLA, I was a member of the Fellowship of Christian Athletes (FCA). We met monthly for lunch, prayer, a Bible lesson, and general camaraderie. Coach Wooden, being a man of faith, would frequent these gatherings, and I was fortunate to be introduced to him by my track coach, Jim Bush (a Hall-of-Famer in his own right). Wooden and I would bump into each other from time to time – our interactions were always brief, respectful, yet insightful.

One particular conversation with Coach Wooden, seemingly ordinary at first, would set in motion a series of events that would alter the course of my life forever. We were discussing injuries. I was on the back end of recovery from a pulled hamstring, which for a track athlete is as demoralizing as it is debilitating. Feeling the irritation of impatience toward the healing process, I expressed to him my frustration. "Obstacles are inevitable," said Coach Wooden, "and the key to navigating obstacles is how you choose to respond. You get to choose your attitude and how you deal with injuries, which is true in all of life. Your response is your choice. By chance, have you read the book, *Man's Search for Meaning* by Victor Frankl?"

I hadn't. Reluctantly intrigued, I went and bought a copy. I'd been reading other books in a similar genre, but many of them were either too esoteric or too focused on the author slash guru rather than on practical, real-world application. However, once I read the description on the back cover, my reluctance quickly faded.

Victor Frankl was a practicing psychiatrist in Austria during the late 1930s and early 40s. Being of Jewish descent when the Nazis invaded, he along with his family were sentenced to the concentration camps in 1942. His father, mother, brother, pregnant wife, and unborn child perished. Over the course of three years, Frankl somehow managed to survive four different camps. Utilizing his clinical skills, he secretly documented on stolen scraps of paper the brutal experience of the camps and how his fellow prisoners dealt with the hardship.

"The experiences of camp life show that man does not have a choice of action... that everything can be taken from a man but one thing: the last of the human freedoms – to choose one's attitude in any given set of circumstances, to choose one's own way."

Frankl's testimony categorically shifted how I saw the world and how I viewed my own life. The first thing that got my attention was the dramatic difference between how Frankl and some small groups of prisoners responded to their situation differently than others. After the initial shock of their internment, which was natural for all of the prisoners to experience, those who were initially spared the gas chambers faced A crucial choice: Accept The responsibility of the suffering and confront it or allow the hopelessness of the situation to determine one's attitude and fate. Those who intentionally chose to bear their burden of suffering were able to find meaning in their actions, even when it cost them their lives.

"And there were always choices to make. Every day, every hour, offered the opportunity to make a decision, a decision which determined whether you would or would not submit to those powers which threatened to rob you of your very self, your inner freedom; which determined whether or not you would become the plaything of circumstance, renouncing freedom and dignity to become molded into the form of the typical inmate."

The second thing that got my attention was the difference between Frankl and me. There I was in sunny Southern California at a prestigious university on scholarship for a sport I loved competing in, making great friends and having good times. Though my life up to that point wasn't without hardship, I weighed my attributes, character, and experience against Frankl's and found myself desperately lacking. Frankel had a toughness, strength, and empathy toward others that I simply did not have. His book challenged me in the deepest possible way to ask, "How does a person build mental toughness and emotional resilience, especially in the face of such cruelty? How do you connect with others in a meaningful way, even under harsh conditions? How do you become someone who responds with inner strength and courage in the midst of adversity? How do you become that person?"

> *"In the final analysis it becomes clear that the sort of person the prisoner became was the result of an inner decision, and not the result of camp influences alone. Fundamentally, therefore, any man can, even under such circumstances, decide what shall become of him – mentally and spiritually. He may retain his human dignity even in a concentration camp."*

So, I continued to explore these questions while at UCLA. Though my formal major was history, my informal study was of these various topics and how they applied to the human condition. Even beyond graduation, I continued my support of a better understanding of how inner strength and resilience play a role in how people go about life and work. I also took a job as an assistant football and track coach at a high school in Los Angeles, which afforded me the opportunity to see how the principles and practices I was learning applied to leading, coaching, and building winning teams. As I matured and got into the marketplace, I began to see the same principles at work in high performance companies. Elite leaders created a culture in those businesses where those principles were taught and encouraged, thus driving their success year after year.

It was now time for me to step into the arena. I started a training and consulting firm, Focus 3, that specializes in helping organizations develop their leaders, build their culture, and equip their employees with the skills to drive performance. Over the years our company has evolved, moved, and developed new products and services, but our core training system continues to be *The R Factor®*. For more than three decades, my colleagues and I have had the great privilege of teaching *The R Factor®* to businesses, nonprofits, public and private schools, college and professional sports teams. Whether here in the United states or across the globe, everywhere we've taught *The R Factor®*, the impact has been profound.

Throughout this book we'll teach you the principles of *The R Factor*® and also share stories about people who applied the disciplines in various circumstances. The purpose for these testimonials is to paint the picture for you to see how these skills helped people navigate and overcome the challenges they faced. Whether you're dealing with a similar situation or find yourself in a comparable circumstance, these examples can help you clarify what responses to engage and mistakes to avoid, so you can confidently work towards your desired outcome. To respect their requests of privacy, some of the names have been changed.

One of the most fulfilling thoughts we receive feedback about is people sharing *The R Factor*® with their families. Spouses and partners not only see improvement in their relationships, but also see the benefits of teaching it to their children. Kids and teenagers have learned that regardless of the situations they face at school, with friends, in sports and other extracurriculars, they always have a choice in how they respond.

The R Factor® then, is a call to action to convert ideas into behavior and knowledge into skill. It's about learning to apply the disciplines that will enable you to breakthrough self limiting barriers so you can experience higher levels of achievement and deeper levels of meaning in work and in life.

Introduction

"Take the first step in faith. You don't have to see the whole staircase, just take the first step."

- Martin Luther King Jr.

How do you know a single decision is going to change your life?

The truth is you don't.

You just say *yes*.

And if you're like me, you say it with your heart in your throat, your bank account nearly empty, and your soul fully awake for the first time in a long time.

That's how this story starts – not with a plan, not with a blueprint – but with a yes.

It wasn't that I had all the answers. I didn't know how to buy a company based on Intellectual Property. I didn't know how to raise capital or secure funding or draft a business plan that would convince someone to say, "Yes, we believe in you." How was I going to scale a business around a framework that had changed my life but was still, to many, just a "leadership tool?"

But I knew how to take one step.

And then another.

And then let the staircase appear, just as Martin Luther King Jr. said it would.

This book is about *that* – about the courage to take one step when you have no idea what's coming next. About learning to listen when the universe, or God, or that still small voice inside you says, *there's more for you. You have a bigger purpose.*

But to really understand how *The R Factor®* found its way into my heart – and eventually into my hands – you have to know where I come from.

—∽—

I grew up with little to no money. Many times, we had little to no food. But what we had was a fierce kind of love, an unshakable loyalty, and a deep commitment to each other. It was something that couldn't be bought.

My mom and dad were both alcoholics during my early years. During those years, life felt uncertain most of the time.

I remember lying in bed and dreaming that my *real family* (a royal family, naturally) would come find me, scoop me up, and take me away to a place with food, warm clothes, and a bedroom just for me. In that dream, I wasn't just rescued, I was seen.

My mom got sober when I was 3. It took my dad a while longer. In fact, I was 12 when he finally got sober. But my mom never left him. "Heather," she'd say, "your dad is sick right now, but he will get well. He will come home." And she was right – he did. Before I turned 13, we packed up everything we owned into a station wagon and a U-Haul and moved from the Boston suburbs to the San Fernando Valley in California. A fresh start.

We didn't have much, but we had each other. And we had a dog named Toto, a Cairn Terrier who followed my mom like a second shadow.

That cross-country drive remains one of my fondest memories. Two weeks on the road, seeing the beauty of this country, cracking jokes in the backseat with my brothers, Scott and David, and laughing so hard we cried. We were, and still are, a unit built on trust and loyalty. Where one goes, we all go.

When I think back to that time, I realize that it wasn't the lack of money that shaped me. It was the presence of resilience and determination.

Our first Christmas in California I had just turned 13 years old. A local church brought food to our front door. I remember standing behind my dad when he opened it, trying to disappear into the shadows, both grateful and a little ashamed. Inside one of the bags was a sack of apples – bright, red, shiny apples.

That may not seem like much. But for me, it was everything. Apples were my favorite, and this bag was *mine.* I didn't have to share. I didn't have to pretend I wasn't hungry. In that moment, I felt abundance for the first time. I felt *chosen.*

It's funny, the things we carry. To this day, I still have what my mom called a "bottomless pit" when it comes to food and, as I later discovered, when it comes to learning, growing, and wanting *more* from life. Not more in the greedy sense. More in the *I-know-there's-something-bigger-out-there* sense.

That's how I've lived ever since. Hungry for growth. Hungry for truth. Hungry to be part of something that matters.

Throughout my life, my mom shared many words of wisdom. Several of her favorite sayings were:

- "Where you are anywhere is where you are everywhere."
- "What if everyone…"
- "When you leave this house, you represent this family."

- "Always leave things better than you found them."

When it came specifically to family, she would say:

- "There are very few people in the world who will be there for you when you need them. Those people are in this family. Never let anything come between us."

That kind of loyalty is rare. Fierce. Sacred.

It's also what carried me through every job I ever held, every leadership position I ever stepped into, and every hard moment that tried to knock me down. My North Star has always been trust and loyalty. That's the real wealth I grew up with along with my mother's voice always speaking to me.

I've come to believe that where there is love and loyalty, there is always a way forward – even when the road ahead is unclear or not visible at all!

Fast forward 30 years – I'm working as an independent contractor in the insurance and financial services industry, attending leadership conferences and chasing results in a culture that often felt… broken.

Then came February 2017. I was in Dallas, Texas in a ballroom packed with 600 people for our annual leadership conference. That's when I heard Tim Kight speak for the first time. He took the stage and shared something called *The R*

Factor®, a system for managing your response to life's events in order to get better results.

It was like lightning struck me. Every word, every slide, every story – *this was it.* This was the language I'd been searching for my whole life. The framework that gave meaning to the chaos, structure to the emotion, and ownership to the outcomes.

When the room stayed silent at the end of Tim's talk, I stood up to applaud. Just me and one other friend across the room, Derek Avera. We locked eyes and shared a knowing glance. *Finally.* Someone got it.

A year later, Tim came back to speak on *The Edge.* This is an idea that we all, at some point, reach a moment in life where we're called to get better. Not because we're broken, but because there's *more* in us waiting to rise.

I didn't just want to know *The R Factor®*, I wanted to live it, teach it, embody it. I signed up for the train the trainer certification immediately. Not everyone did. But I couldn't get enough. The bottomless pit in me wanted to master this system.

As if I wasn't captivated enough by *The R Factor®* the concept of "The Edge" literally had me on the edge of my seat. Tim spoke these words: "Pursuing the best version of yourself is about your commitment to accepting the challenge and achieving a breakthrough at "The Edge." Genetics shape you, circumstances influence you, your choices define you."

—∾—

A few years later, my friend Derek joined the Focus 3 team as a consultant. It was a dream come true for him. And then COVID hit. And Tim Kight, the founder, the voice, and the heartbeat of *The R Factor®*, was diagnosed with Stage 4 prostate cancer.

I followed his journey closely. Derek kept me updated. Tim was fighting, leading, and still embodying what he taught. But the company's future became uncertain. Would the content survive? Would the team stay together? Would the mission carry on and who would do it?

Then came the moment I'll never forget. October 2023. My husband John and I were in Seattle with Derek and his wife, Tania. Over dinner, Derek mentioned that Tim was starting to entertain offers to sell the company, and there were many interested buyers. I couldn't sleep that night.

I remember looking at my phone. It was 3:33 a.m., and I whispered the question to the ceiling: *What about me?*

I loved this content. I believed in it with everything in me. I knew it had impacted my life in a profound way, and it could impact and influence so many more. I couldn't shake the thought: *What if I bought Focus 3?*

When I finally blurted out the idea to my husband that morning, I could see the shock in his eyes. We had just paid off our house. We were finally completely debt free. We were preparing for retirement and plans for slowing down in a few years.

And now I was suggesting we risk it all?

But John, who knows me better than anyone in the world, looked at me and said, "If this is what you really want to do, I know you'll be the best at it. I trust you."

That's trust and loyalty. That's the kind of "ride or die" loyalty, unconditional love and faith he had in me. If I was committed to doing this, then he was all-in, and we were going to do this together. And we've never looked back.

Fifteen months later, I'm sitting at my computer, typing the introduction to this book thinking that this wild, beautiful journey started with a whisper in the dark and led to an entire company, a team I now call my "Incredibles," and a mission that is bigger than all of us.

—∞—

During the eight months I got to spend with Tim prior to his passing, pouring over content, plans and projections, the topic of "*The R Factor®* book" came up several times. For various reasons, Tim never wrote "the book." Everyone around him was pressuring him to write it, but needless to say, he never did. The part that he did write is included at the start of this book, From the Pen of Tim Kight. When he gave that part to me, it felt more like a burden than a gift. He didn't say it outright, but the message was loud and clear. You've got to finish this.

And let me tell you, I wasn't happy. I even shared that with the team. I told them I was irritated because I never wanted this. I never planned for this. And yet, there it was, sitting in my lap like a baby someone had placed in my arms and walked away.

After the acquisition, the requests started pouring in: *What about The R Factor® book? Are you going to finish it? When is the book coming out? When can we read the story?* I didn't even know if there *was* a book. At that point, all I had was Tim's prologue. From there it got put on a back burner, and I hoped it would just "go away."

The truth is that I never set out to write a book. I had never once dreamed of becoming an author. It wasn't in my blood. I wasn't the person with journals stacked under the bed or a vision board with "bestseller" scribbled across it.

But life, in its perfect chaos, intervened.

It started with Ethan. He was a young man I brought onto the Focus 3 team immediately after the acquisition. He was one of my first hires. During our interview, he told me he had written a book.

"You wrote a book?" I asked, raising an eyebrow. I couldn't hide my surprise. I peppered him with questions. "What made you decide to write a book? How did you do that? Who helped you?" He said he had worked with Scriptor Publishing Group, and that's how I met Kelli, the editor who helped me get this book completed. That one conversation with Ethan led me to a connection that turned out to be divine.

On our first Zoom call I tried to convince Kelli I didn't have a book, mostly because I didn't want to write the book. I told her, "I don't know if I have a book. I have a workbook. I have training materials. But I'm not sure that's enough." The whole time I was trying so hard to convince her that I didn't have a book. I listed every reason why I wasn't a writer. I explained all the ways I didn't fit the mold.

She smiled, asked me a few questions, and after an hour of my rambling she said, "Heather, not only do you have a book, you have a story that people need to hear."

That moment cracked something open in me.

After I hung up the call with Kelli, I picked up the phone and called my dad.

"Well," I said, "apparently I have a book."

He paused for a moment. Then said quietly, "Really?"

My precious, wonderful dad. He was living in California, and I was in Texas. We were having weekly family calls to touch base and keep him updated on the company progress. When I am challenged and need someone to listen and provide practical, sound advice, I call my dad. He is an incredible listener and a man of few words. I shared with him the pressure I was feeling. I told him how frustrated I was. How this was supposed to be Tim's book. It wasn't fair. He was the one who wanted it. He should have written it. I explained how uncomfortable I was with the idea of being the one to write it. After all, it wasn't my content. I purchased it, but I didn't create it. At one point I said, out of frustration, "I just don't understand why Tim didn't just write the book."

My dad, after patiently listening to me go on and on for some time, looked at me on that Zoom call from Texas to California and said, "Sweetheart, don't you see? Tim was never supposed to write the book. You were! It was never his book to write. It was always *your* book."

Once again, my dad knew exactly what to say! The silence that followed seemed to last forever. And there it was again, "The Edge," calling me to another level. I burst into tears because in that instant, everything made sense. The delay. The resistance. The 17 pages. All of it. It wasn't about fulfilling Tim's vision. It was about honoring what had always been mine to carry.

If Tim had written it, it would have been technical, smart, polished, and safe. Maybe even a little guarded. It wouldn't have been raw. It wouldn't have been as transparent. It wouldn't have held the truth about struggle or pain or redemption. It wouldn't have revealed the places we fall apart and what it takes to put ourselves back together.

My dad saw it all so clearly. As a recovering alcoholic, grounded in his Alcoholics Anonymous journey, deeply spiritual, and beautifully present in crisis. If anyone lives *The R Factor*®, it's him. Press pause. Get your mind right. Step up. My dad is always calm in the storm. And in that moment, he was exactly what I needed and said exactly what I needed to hear.

When I shared that story with the team, even my Navy SEALs were tearing up. Grown men. Battle-hardened. Sitting around the table with tears in their eyes. Because this wasn't just a book anymore. It was a story about stepping into something you didn't choose, but were chosen for.

And yes, I still call myself the most reluctant author on the planet. However, I carry that title with gratitude. This story, this book, isn't about being polished. It's about being real. It's about "the edge" that life calls you to when you're finally ready to say yes.

Even if you didn't see it coming.

Even if it wasn't part of your plan.

Especially then.

And so, here we are.

This book isn't about me, not really. It's about what's possible when you take the first step. When you trust your gut. When you choose to believe that you were made for more, even when the road ahead is unclear, you step up to "The Edge" and jump!

The R Factor® changed my life. It gave language to my values, structure to my leadership, and clarity to my mission. And now, I hope it does the same for you.

This isn't just a framework. It's a way of being. It's how we lead, how we live, how we love. It's what happens when we stop *reacting* to life and start *responding* with intention.

So wherever you are in your story, on the edge, in the middle, or wondering if you'll ever find your path, I want to invite you into this one.

This book, *The R Factor®*, honors Tim. It honors the system, the disciplines, the testimonials and the content he created over decades. But more than anything, it's a story of my life. I've tried to weave a story through every principle so that you, the reader, can better understand it. My hope is that you can relate to my stories and that you can see the way your own stories fit in. It's not a leadership manual so much as it is a journey.

Let's take that journey together.

The R Factor®

Life comes at us fast. Situations, people, responsibilities, problems, opportunities, change...we are constantly dealing with the *stuff* of life. This presents a universal challenge for every organization and individual:

How do we navigate situations in a way that produces the best possible results?

The answer lies in implementing a simple and powerful framework for being intentional about the way you think, make decisions, and take action.

E + R = O

Event + Response = Outcome

The key to producing outcomes is not the events or circumstances you encounter, but how you choose to respond. It's called *The R Factor®*.

Circumstances are a factor in your life, but they are not the deciding factor. How you manage the R is the difference between proactively choosing your path or living at the mercy of situations you face.

You are constantly making R Factor decisions. Every day you choose how to respond to events you experience and outcomes you want to achieve. You choose what actions you will take (or not take) In pursuit of your goals. You choose whether to give up or persevere through obstacles you encounter. You choose how to interact with people at work and family at home. You choose whether your attitude is discipline-driven or default-driven.

The choices you make are the most powerful factor in your journey through life.

E+R=O will always tell you the truth if you have the courage to listen.

The R Factor® Mindset

The R Factor® is a mindset first and a skill set second. If you do not adopt the mindset, there is a good chance you will not do the work to build the skill set.

The R Factor® Mindset presents itself in four ways:

1. I do not control events. Events come along for all of us. Some are professional, others are personal. Some are bigger than others while there are positive, neutral and negative events. But regardless, we do not control these events. This is hard for so many people who are control enthusiasts and are convinced they control more than they really do. Hopefully, this truth is not bad news to you. If it is, here is the good news…
2. My response is my choice. When one realizes, no matter how difficult the event, I get to choose my response, good things flow from that disciplined response. When you see E+R=O, a key thought should be, "I get to choose my response. Every single time."
3. Outcomes are earned by the quality of my response. If you want a better outcome, choose a better response. Your outcome is often a commentary on the quality of your response.
4. Event + Response = Outcome is simply the way life works. It is our job to get good at it. We live in a

cause-and-effect world. There is a relationship between cause and effect and that relationship can be expressed through E+R=O.

"I do not control events."

Every day you will experience a variety of events that will challenge you. You have the power to influence events and situations, but you do not control them. There will always be things outside of your control that you will have to deal with. Do not give energy to things you do not control.

"My response is my choice."

You are responsible for your decisions and behavior. Events will have an impact on you, but they do not choose for you. Take ownership of your choices and actions, regardless of circumstance. Do not equate having to make a difficult choice with not having a choice. You always have a choice

"I earn outcomes by the quality of my response."

The outcomes you get are determined by the responses you choose. If you want a better outcome, choose a better response. What you do (or don't do) makes a difference. Accept that you will not always get the outcome you want in every situation. There is no magic "R." Many outcomes, especially important ones, require significant time, effort and energy to achieve.

"E+R=O is the way life works."

E+R=O is the cause-and-effect nature of the world in which you live. Your job is to get good at applying it. Don't let other people's impulsive reactions pull you into default, and don't let negative circumstances discourage you. Understand that managing the R with discipline will, over time, result in better outcomes for you and those around you.

The R Factor® **is a mindset first and a skill set second. If you don't adopt the mindset, there's a good chance you won't do the work to build the skill set.**

The R Factor® Skill Set

In this book, you will find a toolbox containing six disciplines for managing the R with intention, purpose, and skill. The daily application of these disciplines determines the quality of outcomes you produce.

Below are brief descriptions of the six disciplines. We will be going into each of these much more deeply in the chapters that follow. In addition, we will share real-life examples and stories so you can see how to apply these same skills in your everyday life.

R1: Press Pause

Press Pause means that before you respond, think and gain clarity. Slow down impulse, get off autopilot, and escape the grip of ineffective habits. Clarify the E (Event) you have, the O (Outcome) you want, and the R (Response) you need. When an event comes into your 20 Square Feet, press pause for clarity… initially, to gain clarity around the event itself. Sometimes this is very easy; other times it is extremely difficult. Once there is exceptional clarity relative to the event, in a disciplined approach, fast forward to gain clarity around the outcome. The more you build these R Factor® muscles, the more frequently the response becomes self-evident.

R2: Get Your Mind Right

Once you've pressed pause, the next step is to get your mind right. This helps you create the appropriate energy for whatever event is in front of you. How many times has this happened? You walk into work knowing you need to knock out a key task for the first hour of your day, and you have generated the right energy to tackle it. But ten minutes into the task, a "hair on fire" emergency grabs your attention. So, you ramp down the energy for the first task and ramp up the appropriate energy for the emergency. Once you put that emergency to bed, you still have 50 minutes left on your original task and need to ramp up that energy again. This goes on all day long among professional people.

When you create a disciplined mindset, it energizes you to respond effectively to the situations you experience. Know how to get into a productive mental state, and how to get out of a negative one. Harness your emotions to work for you, not against you.

R3: Step Up

Only after you have pressed pause and gotten your mind right are you well positioned to step up, which is code for action. To be crystal clear, there is a disciplined action called a response. On the other hand, there is a default action called a reaction. Respond and react are not synonyms. While many people use those terms as synonyms, they are not the same. You do not want a doctor to say, "Your body is reacting to the medicine." Instead, what you want to hear from the mouth of a doctor is "Your body is responding to the medicine."

Take the action required for the outcome you want. Step up and do what needs to be done. When the situation demands it, elevate your R. Your response is most important when the event is most challenging.

R4: Adjust & Adapt

The first three principles need to happen every time an event comes into your 20 Square Feet. There will be many times when we need to adjust, adapt and course correct. Every time? No. But many times in this world we live in. Are you willing to be flexible in the face of changing events and/or outcomes that are not exactly what you want? Will you flex to be the best version of yourself? Will you flex to communicate with people the way in which they prefer?

Things change, so be flexible. As you make decisions and take action, monitor the outcome and adjust appropriately. If you aren't getting the O you want, don't blame the E, change your R.

R5: Make a Difference

While the first four principles are internally focused, this is where a shift occurs. Here the focus goes from internal to external and we confront this significant truth: your response is an event for someone else. When you respond in a disciplined way, with skill, grace and poise, it creates a positive event for the people around you, professionally and/or personal. Conversely, if you react on default, it produces a negative event for those same people. In other words, your R is an E for others. Pay attention to the impact you are having on the organization where you work and the people around you. Manage your attitude, action, and words to maximize your impact.

R6: Build Skill

For most people, building skill in areas where they are already naturally gifted or talented is not that hard. Some things we naturally lean into. But make no mistake: everyone will be asked to build skill in some ways that do not come naturally or easily. What do you do in those moments? Most people shy away and convince themselves it is too difficult, too uncomfortable, too risky to move forward. They are afraid of failure. But elite people embrace those opportunities to improve themselves.

> *Key takeaway: Over time, you can execute these principles with skill, under pressure. But it takes focused repetitions to build these R Factor muscles. There are no shortcuts.*

Develop *The R Factor®* habits and skills necessary for the life you want. R6 is the discipline that determines the level of competence you build in the other five. Pursuing the best version of you is about growth.

Before we look at these more closely, I'd like to introduce you to what we at Focus 3 call our "Three Big Rocks." Understanding these rocks and how they work provides a foundation for developing *The R Factor®* skill set.

Can you imagine living a life focused on these six words – clarity, energy, action, flexibility, impact and growth? That sounds like the best version of you.

The Performance Pathway & Our Three Big Rocks

The R Factor® is a time-tested system based on timeless truths. Let's begin by looking at The Performance Pathway.

The Performance Pathway

This describes the relationship between leadership, culture and behavior…and how they work together to drive results. An accurate subtitle or subheading would be "The Physics of Organizational Behavior." It's simply the way organizations function or operate. So the relationship between the three components and the way they drive results can be very positive or very negative, with lots of points in between.

Think about a for-profit business doing great things – making good money while taking good care of their employees and clients or customers. But also think about a company desperately trying to make money but struggling to keep the lights on. Think about a winning team versus a losing team. How about a school district with a dynamite culture where everyone enjoys being there…the adults like working there and the students have fun while learning there. Finally, consider a hospital with a winning culture as opposed to a hospital with a toxic, dysfunctional culture you can feel when you walk into the building.

All of those different organizations and countless others operate this way: *Leaders create the culture that drives the behavior that produces results.* We can reverse engineer this pathway and it's actually quite easy. If you want better results, what do you need? Better behavior. Better behavior comes from better culture. A better culture comes from more effective leadership.

There's a built-in feedback loop between culture and behavior. Yes, it's a truism that culture drives behavior but it's also true that the behavior within an organization reinforces its culture. Too many organizations have "poster culture." They proclaim the culture they want on a poster or a series of posters down a key hallway. And sometimes the poster(s) do a good job of reflecting the culture of the organization because people behave in a way that is congruent with the language on the poster. But all too often, the poster doesn't represent the organization's culture at all because no one behaves that way.

Here's a key question: can you think of a single important result within your organization that's not directly related to people's behavior? The vast majority of people cannot. It's a great question when opening a conversation regarding behavior. There's so much talk in our world today about leadership, and rightfully so. The same can be said about culture. But there is so little talk about behavior. And when there is talk of behavior, the conversation typically flows in the wrong direction. "What can we do to hedge our bets against the behavior we don't want?" As opposed to "How can we create the culture that will drive the behavior that we do want?"

If we plan to discuss behavior in this book, and we do, then let's start and discuss culture because, again, culture drives behavior. Culture is not built by what you proclaim or preach. It's just not. It would be awesome if we could build culture that way. Just get a group of really sharp people in a room and have them commit to stay there long enough and talk about culture loudly enough that we simply speak into existence the type of culture we want. But it doesn't work that way...it's not nearly that easy.

Instead, culture is built by what we practice, promote and permit. And keep in mind this very powerful truth: if you permit it, you promote it. Consider the culture of your team and organization. Your culture will only be as strong as the weakest behavior you choose to permit. Or allow. Or tolerate. Your team will never become something that its members are not.

Key takeaway: Winning behavior will not survive in a culture that does not support it.

Ultimately, culture is a summation of shared beliefs, the behaviors we're committed to in support of those beliefs, and the combination of beliefs and behaviors should yield certain outcomes. One can consider these desired outcomes. And there is another interesting point connected to these words. On an individual level, one's core beliefs (or values), the behaviors he/she is committed to and the outcomes one wants to deliver to others – that is a solid definition of character. But when it is shared – shared beliefs or values, shared behavioral norms that are expected and accepted, and a shared sense of outcomes – those are the primary pieces that makes up a team's or organization's culture.

The word "core" comes from a Latin root word, and it means "heart." When an individual, a team or an organization says, "These are our core beliefs" what is being said is these are the beliefs we hold close to our heart. Later in this book, we will discuss the importance of acting with courage. That word means "strength of heart." Therefore, to encourage someone simply means to provide strength of heart to another person. To discourage someone means to take away their strength of heart. There is quite enough discouraging action and language in our world today. May we encourage rather than discourage others in our speech and actions. *The R Factor®* is a systematic way to do just that on a consistent basis.

Additionally, think about culture as a journey with key transfers. Often culture starts with a document, and the initial transfer is from paper to head. Members of an organization read the document, let it marinate, and process it over time. And that is a key transfer. But the much more important transfer takes place between head and heart. Buy-in happens in the head. Beyond buy-in is what we are hoping for when it comes to adopting culture. Beyond buy-in is believe-in, and believe-in happens in the heart. There is a profound difference in understanding something in your head versus believing it in your heart and letting it guide your behavior.

Steven Covey, author of "The 7 Habits of Highly Effective People," uses an analogy of big rocks to explain the importance of focusing on the major tasks first. Picture a jar filled with rocks, pebbles, and sand. If you start with the sand, there's no room for the rocks.

But if you place the big rocks in first, you can fit everything else around them. At Focus 3, we have 3 big rocks:

- 20 Square Feet
- Discipline over Default
- No BCD

Rock #1: Own Your 20 Square Feet

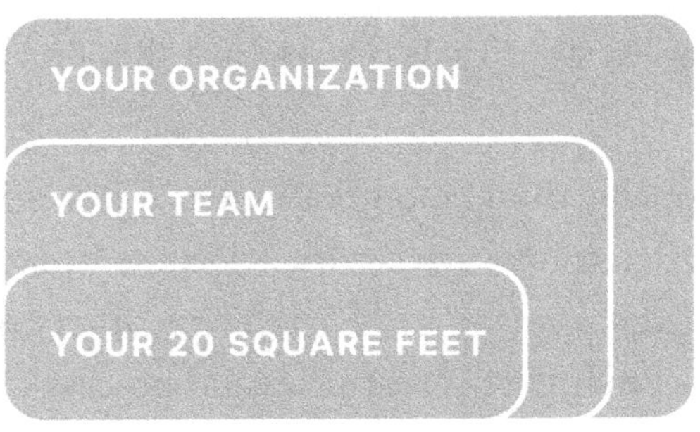

This is simply a metaphor for your sphere of ownership within an organization. Or perhaps better said, it is a metaphor for your sphere of ownership of the culture within the organization. No one controls what you do, nor do you control what anyone else does. So the two important words inside one's 20 Square Feet are ownership and control. Now outside one's 20 Square Feet, the key words are impact and influence. In other words, each day we have the opportunity to impact and influence the people around us, especially at a team level. And in many organizations, what we do on a daily basis affects people at an overall organizational level as well. By the same token, those same people affect our 20 Square Feet each day. Again, that is how culture is built – 20 Square Feet at a time.

Key takeaway: You don't control anyone else's 20 Square Feet and they do not control yours. But you absolutely impact and influence others, just as they impact and influence you.

There is another level to 20 Square Feet as well. Yes, clearly it has professional application but can be applied on a personal level as well. Phrased another way, your 20 Square Feet travels with you. Yes, you own 20 Square Feet of your workplace but you also own 20 Square Feet of your family. Your family has a culture, every family does. You own 20 Square Feet of it. You own 20 Square Feet of your marriage and relationships. You own 20 Square Feet of the community and country where you live. When you travel, you own 20 Square Feet of the freeway, the highway, the airport, etc. Suffice it to say – your 20 Square Feet travels with you.

Inside our 20 Square Feet, all day long every day, we make decisions. We make choices. We are defined by our choices. You make certain choices and those choices make you. One of the most significant choices we make each day is just how elite we choose to be. And it absolutely is a choice. Focus 3 defines elite simply as "the best version of you." How does one become elite? By being better today than yesterday, better tomorrow than today. It is the cumulative impact of what you do day after day. So stack one good day on top of another, on top of another. In building skill the right way, there are no quantum leaps, nor shortcuts.

There is no such thing as a culturally neutral attitude or action.

You don't control the whole world. You never will. But you *do* control what happens inside your 20 Square Feet. And the way you show up in that space creates ripples. Outside of it, you may not have control, but you still have *impact* and *influence*. And whether you realize it or not, you're always making a mark on the world. There's no such thing as a neutral presence. You're either lifting the room or draining it. You're either building trust or breaking it.

Today's challenge: Most people focus on what's happening outside of their 20 square feet

So, the question becomes: What kind of impact are you choosing to make? And how will you own your 20 Square Feet?

Key takeaway: Growth happens slow, small and daily.

No one had taught me about owning your 20 Square Feet when I was young, but in 1st grade, I *lived* it. Sometimes the lessons that shape us the most come wrapped in tiny moments we almost forget – until we realize they were everything.

I remember like it was yesterday. A little girl in my class was crying. We were six or seven, maybe, with pigtails, peanut butter sandwiches, and playground rules. But this wasn't playground stuff. This was real life showing up in a classroom full of crayons and storybooks. And I could feel it. I could feel that this little girl needed someone to help her.

So I went over and asked if she was okay.

She shared something no child should have to carry alone. There'd been drinking and fighting at home. She was clearly scared as she told me her story. I responded the only way I knew how. I told her the truth. "It's okay," I said. "My parents drink, too. My mom doesn't, but my dad does."

And just like that, the teacher swooped in. I was scolded, told I was out of line, and marched to the principal's office like I'd done something wrong. I didn't understand it at the time. I wasn't trying to stir up trouble. I was just trying to help. That little girl was part of *my* space. She was in my 20 Square Feet. And I felt responsible.

That's what I've come to understand, all these years later. We don't always get to choose what happens in life. But we do get to choose how we *respond*. That's the heart of *The R Factor*®, and that day, I responded by stepping up, not stepping back.

I didn't protest or argue. I just sat quietly in the principal's office, waiting for my mom to arrive. Because I had always been raised to tell the truth. To lead with integrity. To care about the people around me.

When my mom arrived? She didn't hold back. She walked right into that school and stood firm. "If my daughter is in trouble for telling the truth," she said, "then we have a bigger problem here." And I remember so clearly that she turned to me and said, "Heather Ann, you never have to be ashamed of who you are or where you come from. You always tell the truth."

That moment shaped me. Because it wasn't just about defending me. It was about *teaching* me. She was modeling what it looks like to own your 20 Square Feet – not with fear, but with courage and clarity.

Looking back, I see how early the seeds were planted. I was the oldest of three. A leader simply because of my birth order. Sometimes leading my own parents. Sometimes leading by observing what *not* to do. We talk about culture a lot, how every family has one, whether it's healthy or not. Ours was dysfunctional at best. But I learned to pay attention. To take notes. To decide what I wanted *my* future family culture to be like.

Even in first grade, I wanted to make a difference in that little girl's day. And Step 6? *Build Skill.* Every time I paid attention, every time I responded with discipline instead of default, I was building the muscles of leadership. Even when the adults around me didn't always show me how.

So, I've been living *The R Factor®* my whole life. I just didn't know it had a name.

Don't let the frustrations on the outside diminish the fire on the inside.

Rock #2: Discipline Over Default

DISCIPLINE

- Intentional
- On-purpose
- Skillful

DEFAULT

- Impulsive
- On-autopilot
- Resistant

Every day you have a choice about what directs your life: discipline or default. Discipline driven behavior is intentional, purposeful and skillful. Default driven behavior is impulsive, autopilot, and resistant.

There is a line in life. We can operate above that line or fall below that line. That line separates discipline and default.

One of the most important decisions we have in front of us each day is whether to be disciplined in nature – in our thoughts, our speech, our behavior – or to drift into default. None of us drift toward discipline. It is part of the human condition that every last one of us, when we drift, it is toward default. Always. In other words, if we do not choose discipline, default will choose us.

It is important to note the word discipline doesn't mean punishment. Its roots are in the Latin language, and it actually means "student." The same Latin root word gives us our word "disciple." Consider how they are spelled. Discipline, therefore, is learned behavior. It does not come naturally;

it must be taught and trained. Default is what feels natural because our human nature gravitates toward being impulsive, on auto-pilot and resistant. Let's consider each of these default categories:

- People who are impulsive are controlled by their emotions. Not the positive emotions, rather the default ones. And typically, the first one. They think it, they say it. They feel it, they do it. Impulsive individuals tend to be overly emotional and frequently let their feelings cloud their judgement. It is also important to note that we are not anti-emotion. Emotions can be a beautiful gift and should be treasured when channeled properly. Think about emotions this way: they are welcome to come along, but my emotions will take their rightful place in the back seat. I am not going to let them drive. Why? Because emotions are a horrible driver. I am going to drive and my emotions are welcome to join me, but in the back seat.
- People on auto-pilot are the ones controlled by their undisciplined habits. There are lots of people in today's world on cruise control. They are the ones watching the clock, punching a clock, going through the motions, doing the minimum required to get by, checking boxes, etc. As one little boy once put it, "I am just waiting for it to get later." Many people live

their lives that way, giving in to their undisciplined habits.

- Finally, people who are resistant – to growth and to change – are the people controlled by their comfort or their comfort zone. The comfort zone feels great, but nothing grows there. Opportunities to grow and change come along and some people push back on such chances in the name of remaining comfortable. "It is too hard, too risky, yes, too uncomfortable. I will pass."

Key takeaway: Today and in the future, your comfort zone is an illusion.

There is simple language to convey the battle between discipline and default that rages inside all of us each day. Discipline is hard; default is easy. That is one reason default is so popular – not just that it is comfortable, but it's also easy. Here is the other truth, and this rule does not have an exception. Discipline wins; default loses. Every single time.

When people operate with discipline in their 20 Square Feet, they work smarter, team better, learn faster, communicate more clearly, and are more resilient.

When people operate on default, they get hijacked by the power of impulse, caught in the gravitational pull of old habits, and stuck in the ruts and routines of the comfort zone.

Discipline does not mean "punishment." It comes from the Latin word *discipulus*, which means "student." Discipline is learned. It means getting better every day by consistently applying standards and principles to your life. Discipline is not something that someone does to you, it's something you choose to do for yourself.

Discipline-driven people do what's effective, even though it's uncomfortable. Default-driven people do what's comfortable, even though it's ineffective.

Rock #3: No BCD

The ultimate default behavior – and the ultimate culture killer – is BCD…Blaming, Complaining, Defending. It is what most people do when things do not go their way.

They blame someone else or blame the situation. It often reveals a lack of accountability on the part of the blamer.

Here is a shocker: people complain. They complain to other people; they complain about other people. They complain about the event or the situation. In some places, there is social support for complaining. It is how some people connect with other people. They get in little groups to complain about what is going on that they do not like. And the individuals who are really good at complaining recruit others into it. "I'm mad about what is happening and I plan to blow off some steam…will you join me?"

Finally, some people defend their own default behavior. They will say, "Do not come at me that way. I have been here

25 years." As if excellence is a function of longevity. Sometimes it is, of course. Some folks have been in their industry for 25 years and you know what that means? They are really good at their job. Others, however, have been around the same amount of time, but in their case, it means they have been good at hanging onto their job. Those are two very different things.

BCD is selfish, unattractive and insanely expensive. Each person in an organization is tied to a certain level of compensation, so each minute spent BCD-ing costs the organization money. Real dollars flow out of the front door when people burn time in BCD conversations, when in reality, doing just about anything else would be more productive.

BCD never enhanced a relationship, achieved a goal or solved a problem. So do not engage in it. BCD poisons everything it touches. It is toxic on every level.

Instead of BCD, let us seek resolution. In other words, mindset matters. If you are bringing up an issue, fine. Why? If it is to complain about it, that is the very definition of BCD. However, if it is to shine a light on the problem for purposes of trying to solve it, that is seeking resolution and the opposite of BCD.

Keep in mind that not every issue has a resolution, certainly not a quick, easy one at the ready. In these cases, we must learn to act with resilience. When it becomes clear a situation will be with us for a while, let us figure out how to get past it. How do we get around it? Over it? Through it?

And BCD is not meant to be a hammer with which to hit people over the head. Quite the opposite. Elite leaders want to hear the issues. Unfortunately, too many people bring up challenging situations in the form of BCD. Next level leaders can differentiate between the BCD portion of a conversation and the actual issue itself. Therefore, the opposite of BCD is not silence or submission, rather resolution or resilience.

Key takeaway: No one enjoys being around BCD. It does not create a fun place to work. Make every effort to eliminate BCD from your 20 Square Feet.

So let us get rid of any lingering attachment to an entitled mindset that we should not have to deal with things we find frustrating or inconvenient. Other tasks may seem aggravating or irritating and some things simply rub us the wrong way; it is that proverbial burr under our saddle. But no one is immune from such tasks. We all have these boxes to check so approach it with the right attitude. You will get a very funny look if you ask a top leader a question like this: "You just get to do the things you want, right? You only do the fun stuff, correct?" Obviously not. So why should you feel like you are above the things you do not care for? No one gets to pick and choose only the parts of a job they want to do. Enter into such tasks with the proper attitude.

After all, you are the architect of your attitude. Build a good one.

R1: Press Pause

The first of our 6 steps in *The R Factor®* is Press Pause. This step is important to use when emotions flare, where people get triggered, and when the stakes feel personal. It's not just a framework or a concept on a whiteboard, it's how we live our lives, every day, and how we shape the lives of the people around us, whether we realize it or not.

And one of the most powerful tools we have is to Press Pause.

It sounds simple. Almost too simple. But don't let that fool you.

Press Pause is where everything begins. It's the foundation. It's what gives you the *space* between an event and your reaction. It's what turns reactivity into responsiveness. And it's what separates people who live by default… from people who live by *discipline*.

I've said this before in workshops, and I'll say it again here: Imagine a world where more people paused before reacting. Paused and thought about the impact of their words or paused to consider how their actions might ripple outward. If people truly took that moment to press pause between the stimulus and the response… I believe the world would be radically different. Kinder. Safer. More compassionate.

When you consider the threat of almost *any* major failure, personal or societal, you can usually find the moment someone didn't pause. Someone didn't think. Someone reacted from fear, emotion, ego or pain.

Emotions hijack clarity.

And that's what makes Press Pause so essential and so powerful.

Press Pause = Perspective

One of the most important things I've learned is that your R is someone else's E.

Let me say that again: Your Response is an *Event* for someone else.

You might be having a bad morning and snap at your kid or your coworker. You might be running late and get snippy with the Starbucks barista. You might honk at someone in traffic, roll your eyes, post something negative online. And to you, it's just a moment. But to *them*? It might be the thing that lingers all day. It might be the reason they cry in the break room or stop trusting people. It might be the thing that triggers their own default behavior.

Your "R" is an "E" for someone else.

We're all just humans bumping into each other. And every bump leaves a mark – sometimes a bruise, sometimes a blessing. You get to choose.

So when I teach Press Pause, I'm not just talking about behavior management. I'm talking about creating better outcomes both internally and externally. I'm talking about choosing to live with intention instead of impulse and with discipline versus default.

Wayne Dyer said something that has stuck with me for decades: *"When you change the way you look at things, the things you look at change."*

It's all about time, space and perspective. That quote is exactly what Press Pause makes possible. It gives you enough distance to reframe, to adjust your lens, and to shift your focus frame, as we say in *The R Factor*®. If you're walking around thinking the world is against you, that's what you'll see. But if you pause and ask, "What else might be true here?" then *everything* changes. The fact is, you can find evidence to support whatever you believe.

Just because something grabs your attention doesn't mean it deserves your attention.

Bringing it into an example of real life, just imagine this:

You're driving on the highway and the speed limit's 70. You're going the limit when someone comes up behind you riding your bumper like they're trying to merge into your backseat. What do you do?

Well, if you're living in *default*, you brake-check. You flip them off. You let your irritation lead the charge. You give them your worst.

But if you Press Pause?

You ask yourself: *What outcome do I want here? Do I want to get into an accident? Do I want to ruin both our days? Or... do I just want to get where I'm going – safely and on time, or possibly even a few minutes early?*

Then the answer becomes simple: I change lanes. I let them pass.

That doesn't mean they *win* and I *lose*. It means no one has to lose. That's the difference between ego and emotional intelligence. Between reacting and responding.

And that lesson? It goes far beyond traffic.

It's the same in our relationships. Our workplaces. Our communities. Our conversations around money, race, religion, politics, parenting – you name it. The stakes may be different, but the skill is the same.

Every time you choose to Press Pause, you reclaim your power. You realign with whom you want to be. And you give someone else the gift of a better experience, a softer landing, the benefit of the doubt, and a moment of grace.

You change the room, the moment, and sometimes the person.

All because you simply took a breath and pressed pause.

Sometimes how we see the problem *is* the problem.

R2: Get Your Mind Right

From as early as I can remember, my mother would say: *"What you language, so shall it be."*

She believed, with everything in her, that the words we speak shape the lives we live. And not just the words we speak to *others* – but especially the ones we speak to *ourselves*. The conversations we carry inside our own minds are what create the emotional tone for our days, our relationships, and ultimately, our future.

It's amazing the conversations that go on in our heads. I often say, "The mind is like a bad neighborhood. Don't go there alone!" Even worse, at times, if someone spoke to us the way we speak to ourselves, there might be a fight! At Focus 3, we believe this can be the hardest of all the steps because this is where self-talk lives. This is what "get your mind right" is all about.

It's about choosing your mindset on purpose, before the world gives you a reason not to. It's about setting your mental tone like you set the temperature in your home. It's pre-paving your response to life before life comes at you.

I learned this at a very young age.

I was thirteen years old when I got my first real "job." We'd just moved to California, and our family, like many families, was going through a tough time financially. When the lady we rented our house from, Mrs. Botte, offered to "let me" clean her house on Saturdays for ten dollars an hour which my mom accepted immediately on my behalf. She was excited and hopeful. "It's an opportunity for you to make some money for your family," she told me. "Work hard, be polite and remember – when you leave this house, you represent this family."

And I intended to. I was eager to help. I had every reason to feel proud walking into that experience. But what I walked into was something different.

From the moment I got into her car, a gold champagne, beautiful Jaguar, Mrs. Botte made it clear that I wasn't welcome as a *person*. I was there as help. She put a towel down on the seat before I got in. She told me not to "get her car dirty." When we got to the house, she made me change into a different pair of shoes because mine were probably too dirty for her floors. The message was subtle, but it was clear: *You are less than. And you are not to be trusted in my space.*

It got worse.

She criticized how I cleaned and told me I was not very bright for using the wrong cleaning product. She fed me half a sandwich at the kitchen bar while she and her sons sat at the table with a full spread. She treated me like I was invisible and a second class citizen, as if my only value was in scrubbing her floors but not sitting on her furniture.

Everything in me *felt* small. Insignificant. Embarrassed. But even as I stood in her oversized bathroom scrubbing surfaces that hadn't seen care in a while, I could hear my mother's voice:

"Be polite. Represent our family well. This is a good opportunity."

That voice became my *self-talk*. It was my *mindset cycle* in action.

Because here's what I know:

If I had focused on how insulted I felt, how unfair it all was, how hurt and angry I was becoming, my feelings would've taken over. I would've been flooded with resentment and tears. And then my *actions* would've followed that path. Maybe I would've snapped back. Walked out. Slammed a door. Lost my temper. Reacted from pain instead of responding from purpose.

And if I'd done that, I would've forfeited what *I* had control over – my mindset, my behavior, and my integrity and dignity.

Instead, I pressed pause.

At the ripe "old" age of 13, I reminded myself: *This is temporary. This is four hours. I'm doing this for my family. I'm choosing how I want to feel about this – not letting her decide that for me.*

That's what it means to Get Your Mind Right.

There is a mental exercise I use each day called Pre-paving.

When I wake up, I set my intention. I tell myself, "*This is going to be a good day. I'm going to show up with joy. I'm going to be a light.*" Just like my mom told me every morning growing up: "Heather Ann, your job is to spread light and joy."

I've carried that with me ever since. Because mindset isn't something that just *happens* to you. It's a choice. It's a habit. It's the daily discipline of speaking to yourself in a way that lifts you up, so that you can lift others up too.

And sometimes that mindset gets tested. *Really* tested.

When someone speaks to you like you're not worth their time. Or treats you like your dignity is disposable. Or assumes that because you're young or poor or different, you don't matter.

That's when Pressing Pause and Getting Your Mind Right saves the day, and at the very least, the moment. When your self-talk is strong, it fuels healthy emotions. Those emotions lead to actions you can be proud of. That's the *Mindset Cycle*:

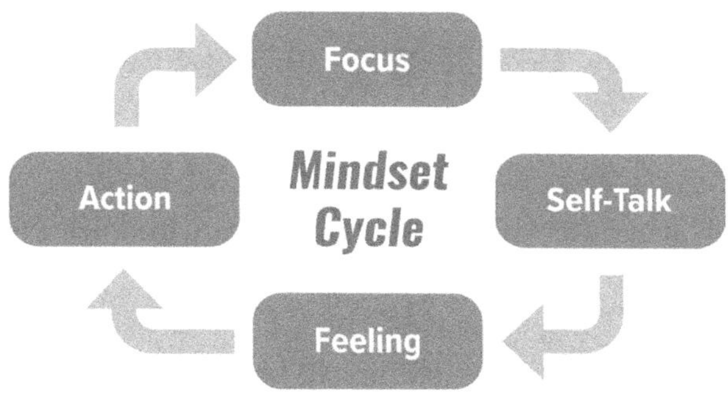

If you want better outcomes in your life, you don't start with what's happening *around* or *outside* you. You start with what's happening *within* you.

For elite people, the Mindset Cycle runs in a disciplined way. For most people, it runs on default.

Too many people walk through life looking to be offended. Looking to be wronged. Looking for reasons to prove they don't belong. Looking for evidence to support a flawed or damaging view.

And I get it. I really do. Especially if you've ever been overlooked, underestimated, or uninvited. When you view your life and the world through that lens, you don't just see the world that way – you *interact* with it that way. And it becomes a self-fulfilling prophecy.

But you can change it.

You can wake up and decide, *Today I'm going to find what's good. I'm going to be the kindest person in the room. I'm going to do my best work, even if no one notices. I'm going to treat people with dignity and respect, even if they don't treat me the same way back.*

Because *you* set the tone in your 20 Square Feet. Not *them.*

You can only do that when you get your mind right.

There is an inverse relationship between emotions and clarity; as emotions run high, clarity is low. Get a handle on your emotions and clarity increases.

R3: Step Up

If you want to win the moment, you have to be in the moment.

That one truth has shaped so many of my decisions, especially the ones that scared me most. Life isn't about waiting for all the lights to be green and your path laid out perfectly before you. It's about responding with discipline, even when your emotions are swirling and the outcome is still a blur in the distance.

As I shared in the introduction, I'll never forget the night I really stepped up. Big John and I were in Seattle having dinner with our dear friends, Derek and Tania. Tim had been battling his diagnosis for years, and for the first time, I saw the fight starting to wear on Derek. He was always so optimistic, so steady. But that night, something shifted. His eyes said what his words couldn't. He was uncertain of the future and what would happen to the company and the entire team, for that matter.

And in the stillness of that night, I heard it, clear as a bell: *You should buy Focus 3.*

It wasn't a thought. It was a certainty and a calling. I shook it off at first. I mean, where did that come from? But it was loud. It was persistent. And it was unmistakably for me to hear.

That's what stepping up looks like. It's not a perfect plan. It's not waiting until conditions are just right. It's hearing the call and choosing to act.

The next morning, I woke up at 5 a.m. (which anyone who knows me knows is *not* my thing). I sat on the floor of our hotel room at the Edgewater, looking out over the water, the sun just beginning to rise. And I couldn't wait for John to wake up. I felt like a kid on Christmas morning. When he opened his eyes, I said it straight out: *I think I'm supposed to buy Focus 3.*

He looked at me, completely stunned. "Can I get a cup of coffee first?"

Fair enough.

We had worked so hard for the past 6 years with intention and focus to pay off our home and become debt free. We had sacrificed and gone without in order to be free. Planning our next chapter with peace and margin. So, of course, it sounded crazy. But I couldn't let it go. I didn't need to have all the answers. I just needed to say yes to the moment in front of me.

For every situation you face, there are discipline-driven responses available to you. And it's your responsibility to Step Up and take the action required to get the outcomes you want. That starts with winning the moment. That means *being* in the moment, not dwelling on the past which creates regret, not worrying about the future which only creates anxiety, but fully focused on what needs to happen right now. In order to win the moment, you must be in the moment.

The only moment available to you is the one you are in right now.

When we met Derek and Tania at the airport on our way home, I could hardly wait to ask, "What would you think if I bought Focus 3?"

Derek didn't even hesitate. "On the scale of worst-case to best imaginable scenario, you buying Focus 3 is off the charts."

There was another piece of evidence and confirmation that I was on the right track!

Did I know what I was doing? Kind of, but not really. Did I know how it would all work out? Not at all. But I took the next disciplined action. And then another. And then another.

That's how you Step Up. You convert impulse into action. You don't get swept away by fear or paralyzed by uncertainty. When things are overwhelming (and they will be) you focus on just one disciplined action at a time. Even when the outcome seems a thousand miles away, you take the next step. That's what turns the dream into a reality.

We hit roadblocks. As I was trying to get funding to purchase the company, eleven banks said no. And then, the twelfth banker, Jody, suggested something that changed everything: "I know this sounds crazy, but have you considered mortgaging your home?" I laughed. We had just paid it off. But maybe, just maybe, that was the plan all along. Preparation before the call. Perhaps that's why we paid our home off.

From there, the doors started opening. Rochelle, an acquisition specialist, was referred to me by Jody, and helped us structure the acquisition. I will be forever grateful to these two "special angels", Jody and Rochelle, for helping me architect the acquisition.

I realized that stepping up wasn't a one-time decision. Stepping up is a *daily* process. The most meaningful outcomes aren't achieved in a single moment. They are built through perseverance and discipline. It's the *cumulative impact* of small, sometimes seemingly insignificant, courageous actions repeated over time. That's what creates transformation.

So no, I wasn't fearless. I was faithful. I showed up when it was easier to stay comfortable. I acted when it would've been simpler to delay. I listened to the voice inside, and I moved, even when the path wasn't clear.

That's what stepping up looks like.

Untether your emotions from your circumstances.

Let me share another moment like that. This one happened after a Focus 3 workshop.

An electrical lineman for one of our clients, attended an R Factor workshop. His job was to ride a small, one-man metal bucket a hundred feet into the air, sometimes during snowstorms, sometimes after hurricanes, to restore power so the rest of us can flip a switch and carry on. It's truly incredible how brave these linemen are!

It's dangerous work. In fact, it could be life threatening work teetering up there in that tiny basket. It's also draining. So every night as he came home physically and mentally exhausted, he kicked off his boots, cracked open a beer, and sank into the recliner with the ballgame on television. And every night, his ten-year-old would race into the room, beaming, "Dad's home! Do you want to play catch"

And every night, the answer was the same: "Later, buddy. Just later."

That "later" became the soundtrack of their relationship.

Tony, one of our Senior Consultants who is a former Navy SEAL, challenged the group to recognize the tiny moments where we choose comfort over connection. Something about it landed. The lineman felt it. He scribbled notes. Made a quiet promise to do better.

That afternoon, it was the same routine. He walked in, grabbed a beer, and settled into his chair. His son came barreling down the hall, full of joy. And just before the old words could leave his mouth, the training echoed in his mind. *Don't miss this moment.*

He set the beer down. Turned off the TV. Looked up at his son and said, "Let's go play catch."

His son froze, stunned. "Hold on, Dad." He sprinted down the hall. "Mom! Something's wrong. Dad wants to play ball!"

His mom came out, half laughing, half in disbelief.

"Nothing's wrong," the lineman said. "I love you, and I'm just working on getting better."

They tossed the ball until the sun disappeared behind the trees, and that night, he wrote us a message: *I left for work an average dad. I came home better. My 30-day challenge starts now. Every day, I choose presence over autopilot and to play catch with my son.*

That's what stepping up looks like. It's not always bold or loud. It's not polished. It's not fearless. But it *is* faithful.

It's turning off the distractions. Saying yes when it's easier to delay. Reaching for connection instead of comfort. Showing up with intention. One moment at a time.

Transformation rarely happens in leaps. It's slow, small and daily.

You don't need the whole staircase. You just need the next step.

Take it.

R4: Adjust and Adapt

We thought we had a home. We had packed up everything and moved across the country from Boston to California for my dad's new position. But when we arrived, the house we were supposed to move into had been rented out from under us. Just like that, we were homeless. We didn't know anyone, and my dad wasn't scheduled to start work for another week. We had nowhere to go.

We ended up in a rundown place called the 99 Palms Motel in Burbank. It was one room with a king bed, a tiny kitchenette, a bathroom and lots of cockroaches that would scatter when you turned on the lights. The five of us – my parents, my two younger brothers, and I – shared that space. We all crammed into the bed at night, taking turns sleeping on the floor. The motel had a pool, which was exciting at first, until it turned green and was condemned by the city within a few weeks.

Meanwhile, my dad showed up to his new job the next week, expecting to step into a familiar role. Instead, he was handed a broom and told he'd be sweeping floors. They said, "We guaranteed a job, not the same job." And then they cut his pay. It was a punch to the gut, and certainly to the wallet.

That was my first real experience with the harsh truth about change. It doesn't wait for you to be ready. It doesn't come with instructions. And it doesn't care how hard you worked for what you thought you'd have or had.

Here's what I've learned since then: **Change is not a threat. It is the bridge to your future.** The discomfort you feel is not danger. It is the old way resisting the new way. That is what makes adjusting and adapting so essential – not just for survival, but for growth.

My brothers and I knew we had to do something. It was summer. We weren't starting school for another six weeks. We had time, we had curiosity, and we had each other. One day, at the grocery store with my mom, we noticed a machine outside where people were turning in aluminum cans for money. That spark of possibility lit something in us. We figured if we could collect cans, we could earn a few dollars.

So we started dumpster diving. Yes, dumpster diving! After all, where else do you find discarded cans? I had just turned 13. My brothers were 10 and 11. We borrowed a shopping cart from Ralph's grocery store, walked up the hill every morning, and got to work. One of us would climb into the dumpster, throw cans out, and the others would catch them. It was disgusting. We were filthy and smelled awful, but we were determined. On our first trip, we earned $11. We proudly brought the money back to the motel and our mom, beaming with pride. When she asked us where we got the money, we proudly shared our ingenuity and hard work. As she listened, my mother broke down in tears. She didn't say anything for a few moments and then asked us to never do that again. The thought of her kids "dumpster diving" was awful and desperate. She didn't like it one bit.

Looking back, I understand that moment so differently now. As kids, we were having fun and felt resourceful. But for my mom, it was a symbol of just how far things had fallen. We didn't actually promise my mom we wouldn't do it. We just didn't tell her so she wouldn't cry. Besides, we needed the money.

Eventually, a firefighter spotted us with our cart and offered us something better. He gave us a crate of empty Coke bottles and told us the store would pay more for them. We returned every few days, and somehow there was always another crate waiting. I think those firefighters started drinking extra soda just to help us out. For all I know, they could have been pouring it down the drain. How could you drink that much Coke? That small act of kindness made a huge impact on our family. One day, they actually drove us to the grocery store in the fire truck! There we were riding in this big, red firetruck like we were in a city-wide parade. We felt so special!

This is what it means to adjust and adapt. When your plans fall apart, when promises aren't kept, and when your comfort zone vanishes, you pivot. You don't wait for things to get easier. You change your mindset and take the next step forward.

Be agile and not fragile.

Resisting change doesn't stop it or make the change go away. It only adds stress. You can either stand still and struggle, or you can move with it and grow. Change is not the enemy. It is the invitation to get better. The mindset you bring to change – not the change itself – determines your level of stress.

Too many people try to hide in the comfort zone. The truth is: your comfort zone is an illusion. While you're sitting still, trying to hold on to what was, the world keeps moving. If you don't adjust and adapt, you don't just stand still – you fall behind.

What we learned that summer in Burbank was more than just how to earn a few dollars from bottles and cans. We learned that even as kids, we had the power to bring value. We learned to think creatively, act resourcefully, and rely on each other. Most importantly, we learned that when life throws you into chaos, your mindset is the first thing you have to lead with.

Change is going to come, whether you are ready or not. But if you embrace it, if you treat it as a bridge instead of a barricade, it will carry you into a stronger version of yourself.

So take a breath, wipe off the grime, and keep going. Adjust. Adapt. And trust that what feels like falling apart is often just the beginning of being rebuilt – stronger, wiser, and more prepared for what's next. Sometimes, just sometimes, when things seem like they are falling apart, they may actually be coming together!

R5: Make a Difference

If there's one thing I know for sure, it's this: your behavior impacts everyone around you. Whether you realize it or not, you are always making a difference – for better or worse – by how you show up. I often say – jokingly, but not really – there are people who light up the room and people who bring the lights down!

We tend to overestimate how others affect us and underestimate how much we affect others. Why? Because we judge ourselves by our intentions, but others experience us through our actions. And that gap, that blind spot, is often where the real work begins.

In every organization, the greatest performance variable isn't the mission statement or the strategy. It's how people behave in their 20 Square Feet. That's your personal sphere of ownership. You can't control everything, but you can control that.

Your attitude, your actions, and your words are your responsibility. And when those three things are in alignment, something powerful happens: you build trust. You gain credibility. You create a ripple effect in your home, your workplace, and your relationships and our world at-large.

We teach this in every workshop. We'll ask: "Of the three – attitude, actions, or words – which is most important?" Most people choose attitude. Some say actions. Almost no one picks words.

I've always chosen words when I've been asked that question because I know that words linger. Words leave a mark.

I once heard a woman say that in a workshop and I'll never forget it. "Words linger," she said through tears. And she was right. Words shape our self-talk. They either build or break our confidence. They are repeated in our minds over and over, long after the words have been spoken and the moment has passed.

I think of all the people I've known who made a difference in my life, not through grand gestures but through simple words and small acts of kindness. One of those people was someone I've always called "my cafeteria angel."

When we moved to California, as you've read, money was tight. I used to walk two miles to school and back. I'd get there before 7 a.m., long before classes began. I loved school. It was always a magical place for me, but the only place open at that hour was the cafeteria.

I'd sit in the back, far away from the smell of breakfast. And then one day, a woman, "my cafeteria angel," walked out from the kitchen. I can still see her hairnet, plain apron, and bright blue eyes. She looked at me and asked, "Honey, are you going to have breakfast today?"

I told her I wasn't hungry, knowing darn well I was. I just didn't want her to know that I didn't have money for breakfast. She just smiled and walked away.

A few minutes later, she came back with a slice of coffee cake and a carton of milk on a little tray. She winked at me and said, "We had some extra and I didn't want it to go to waste." From that day on, she brought me breakfast every single morning that she saw me in the cafeteria. No fanfare. No questions. Just quiet, consistent kindness.

Years later, when I graduated, I bought her a sweater with my babysitting money and gave it to her to say thank you. She cried and said, "You've been an angel to me." She explained that so many of the kids never thanked her or even acknowledged that she was there. Many days she felt invisible. She said seeing me so eager to get to school inspired her, and our kind, brief morning interactions made her feel valued.

Can you believe that?

This woman changed my life with a slice of coffee cake, a carton of milk and her kindness. And still, she felt like the one who had been blessed.

That's the beauty of impact. It's not a one-way street. It's an echo.

You don't have to be extraordinary to make a difference. You just have to be available and willing.

Maybe it's telling your child you're proud of them. Maybe it's looking a stranger in the eye and saying, "I see you." Maybe it's writing the note, sending the card, or just taking a moment to speak a kind truth out loud instead of keeping it to yourself. We're all walking around thinking beautiful things about the people we love, but so few of us actually say them out loud.

I think about Tim. About the moment he looked me in the eyes and said, "You're the one. I believe you're the one to carry this work forward."

He could have kept that thought to himself. But he didn't. He said the words. And they changed everything.

If you want to make a difference, you don't need permission. You don't need a platform.

You just need to start with your words.

Take ownership of your 20 Square Feet. The people in your life feel your presence more than you realize. And when your words, your actions, and your attitude come together, that's when trust is built and cultures shift.

You have no idea how much power you carry.

So pay attention. And make a difference on purpose.

R6: Build Skill

I've only had two W2 real jobs in my life. Even when I worked for someone else, I treated it as if I was self-employed, always building something of my own, challenging myself to be the best at whatever I was doing. Sales, marketing, consulting, recruiting – if there was a mountain to climb, I was already halfway up it before I even knew what gear I needed to be in.

I've always been able to sell anything I believed in, but I was never formally trained in sales. I was just relentlessly curious. I'd absorb everything. Study the best. Push past any self-doubt. Whatever I was doing, I wanted to be the best at it. So I studied the records, the rankings, the benchmarks. I'd ask myself who did it the fastest? Who did it the best? And then I'd set my eyes on doing it faster and better.

That mindset has served me well, but it took me a while to learn it. In fact, I had to go through some hard times before I really understood it. One of those times was when I left home at 15 years of age. My mom and I were having some difficulties and for whatever reason, I thought I was ready to be out on my own and not abide by the house rules. I don't know what I was thinking and looking back, it's one of the biggest regrets I have. Then again, regrets also come with consequences. I left home for two years and during that time, I started to work full-time and went back to school. I was trying to continue my life as usual, but things would later reveal themselves that it wasn't really "usual." I had teachers, educators and friends around me who kept encouraging me to move back home but being a Type A personality (or should I say Triple A type personality), that wasn't my plan.

Then I had another one of those tough life lessons when I was 17. At that time, I was working full-time and going to college. I was trying to prove I could do it all. I wasn't feeling well, but I thought I was just tired because I was so busy. I assumed this was just normal for someone working this hard to make something of themselves. What I didn't know was that I was becoming very sick and near death.

It was November of 1986. The week before Thanksgiving I had taken a job at a collection agency as the receptionist. It was hardly glamorous, but it paid the bills. I answered phones and did numerous tasks. My boss, Rochelle Handy, ran the place. She was tough but kind. She was the kind of woman you don't easily forget.

One morning, Rochelle walked in, took one look at me, and stopped in her tracks.

"Heather, you look green."

I laughed it off. "Maybe it's just the color of this shirt," I said.

But she wasn't laughing. "No, really. You look green. Are you feeling okay?"

I told her I was just tired, and I told myself that, too. That's all it was, right?

The next day, I showed up again. I was tired, and my stomach was cramping. I took a call at my desk, and when I stood up, a pain like lightning ripped through me. I hit the ground. I couldn't breathe, and I couldn't move. When I fell, I hit the glass door to the office behind me. Luckily someone heard me fall and came to see what was happening. They helped me up and sat me in my chair.

I knew I didn't have the money to go to a doctor, so I steadied myself, told everyone I was okay and tried to focus on work. Unfortunately, I continued to feel worse and worse. Eventually, when I went to stand up to leave, I couldn't. The pain was so excruciating that my boss called for an ambulance. I was wheeled into a hospital, and I remember the ER team firing off questions. Was I feeling pain previously? Was I sexually active? Could it be a tubal pregnancy? After a few tests and some pain medication, they sent me home with no diagnosis and told me to come back if it got worse.

That night, I started hemorrhaging. By the time I came back through those sliding glass doors, I was fading. They took me to the nearest hospital. I was 17, alone and scared. Since I was underage, they asked me for an emergency contact. That's when they called my mom. As I lay on the gurney, knees drawn up, belly swelling like I was 8 months pregnant, my mom came rushing in the door to the hospital. I had lost about 4 pints of blood, and my mom wanted to give me her blood for a transfusion. That was around the same time when AIDS was a hot topic, and my mom wanted to be sure I didn't get infected blood through a transfusion. The doctor looked at my mom and said the words I'll never forget. As he stood over me on the gurney, he said, "Having you give blood will take several hours, and she doesn't have fifteen minutes."

Everything seemed to move in slow motion and nearly stopped. My mom's face went pale. Her tears came fast and hard, but I looked at her and whispered, "Not today, Mom. I'm not going to die today. I promise."

They rushed me into surgery. My spleen burst as they opened me up. Twenty hours, 158 stitches, and 80 staples later, I woke up in a morphine haze, confused and weak, in the ICU. Apparently, they had scrubbed and cleaned and pieced me back together. I stayed there for five weeks and didn't leave the hospital until after Christmas.

The first time my dad and brothers came to see me, I was skeletal. Maybe 90 pounds laying in my hospital bed. My dad took one look, muttered, "Oh my God," and walked out. I still remember that clear as day, not because it hurt, but because I finally understood the depth of his heartbreak. We hadn't seen each other in almost two years. I had left home as a young teenager two years ago, and now I was in a hospital bed and had almost died.

The doctor sat at the foot of my bed the day I was released and said something that has shaped every day of my life ever since:

"You can live without a spleen. But your immune system will never be the same. You have to protect your health. You have to sleep. You don't get to run on fumes anymore, Heather."

He warned me. I was the type to go and go and go until my body gave out again. "You're not Superwoman," he said. "You have limits. Listen to them."

It took almost a year to recover. I couldn't walk without help or sit up without pain. My dad used to lay pillows across my abdomen so I could cough without tearing stitches. The scar from my sternum to below my navel is still there. I see it every day as a constant reminder that I am not invincible.

And that scar? That was my first "edge." It showed up uninvited, but it saved me. It brought me home to my parents, to healing, and to reconciliation. It forced me to stop running, stop proving, and start listening.

And here's the thing. I had offers from Ivy League schools. I was in advanced placement classes. I loved to learn. But after that trauma, I never went back to school. Life stopped for a full year. In fact, the recovery swallowed me whole. I laid on my parents' couch for months, learning how to walk, move and live again.

I stayed at home with my parents until I was 22. Maybe that was the right age to leave in the first place. Maybe God had to bring me back in order to send me forward again. But this time He sent me out there whole.

There are edges all throughout life. At work. In marriage. With our kids. In our health, our finances, our faith. Some you walk toward willingly. Others arrive like a punch to the gut. Literally.

What matters is what you do when you reach that edge.

That year, I had to change something. I had to change the way I lived. And I also had to stop the illusion that I could do it all. That was my big breakthrough.

It's amazing how wanting to be fiercely independent and in charge of my life made me realize how much I needed my family. I was young and naïve to think I knew it all. I'm just glad I lived to get smarter!

And so now, when I work with others – leaders, mothers, dreamers – I tell them this. If life is screaming at you, don't wait until you're bleeding out on a gurney. Pay attention when it whispers. Because if you don't, life will find a way to force you to listen.

It always does.

In your journey you will come to "The Edge" which is a key decision point in your personal and professional growth. "The Edge" marks a place where life challenges you to get better. It is called "The Edge" because it's just beyond your current ability. It requires you to stretch, push and get out of your comfort zone in order to build next level skill.

THE EDGE

WHERE YOU ARE NOW	→	WHAT IS POSSIBLE

Throughout your life you will have edges. Some edges will be at work, and others will be at home. Still others will be in your friendships, your fitness, and your finances. Pursuing the best version of you is about your commitment to accepting the challenge and achieving a breakthrough at "The Edge."

How we feel isn't always a good gauge or barometer or what it is we need to do. In those moments, manage the gap.

Genetics shape you. Circumstances influence you. Your choices define you.

Everyone is born with a certain level of talent. However, talent is not the *key* variable in your development and success. It's not what determines your future. The difference-maker is mindset. It's drive. It's your willingness to do the work to get better.

You can protect your ego OR get better. You can't do both.

There are five choices at the heart of building skill and achieving a breakthrough at "The Edge":

1. **Be Relentless in Focus and Effort**

   This one requires no talent. It just means that you need to do the work. Stay consistent. Put in the reps, especially when no one is watching. Many people fail to get better because they get tired or bored of doing reps long before they've mastered the mechanics of the skill. If you don't do the reps, though, you won't build the skill. Persistence is necessary.

2. **Embrace Productive Discomfort**

   Get uncomfortable. That discomfort you feel? That's growth in progress. Reach beyond your comfort zone and practice at the edge of your current abilities. If it doesn't challenge you, it won't make you better.

3. **Use Mistakes as Feedback**

   Mistakes aren't failures. They're information. In fact, there is valuable feedback in the mistakes you make, but only if you choose to seek it out. Mistakes are a natural part of the journey to success, so it's important to leverage them and turn them into an advantage. Learn from them and keep moving. After all, building skill is about progress, not perfection.

4. **Defeat Fear**

   Fear distorts what you see and limits what you do. Another way to look at it, though, is that it's a signal that something meaningful is on the line. Don't think of fear as a stop sign. Acknowledge it and move through it with courage. Courage is the antidote to fear, but it doesn't just happen. You need to build courage over time. As you develop your courage you develop your inner strength so that fear doesn't become a stop sign.

5. **Be Coachable**

   Growth isn't a solo act. We are all limited in how much we can evaluate our own performance and progress. There is only so much we can see of ourselves. That means you need input from others to truly help you grow. Being coachable is the discipline to receive instruction and feedback without getting defensive or making excuses. The more coachable you are, the faster you will get better.

These five choices aren't just ideas. They're disciplines. They're habits. They're how you build the skill that carries you beyond the edge of your current ability.

I've faced an edge more times than I can count. I could've stopped when I didn't know how to recruit. When I was terrified of public speaking. When I'd never run a company based on intellectual property. When I had to write a book. But I didn't. I kept going. I leaned in. I said yes.

When I bought Focus 3, I wasn't buying a building or a product. I was buying content and curriculum. I had to figure out not just how to buy it, but how to scale it. That was a new kind of edge. But even in that uncertainty, I felt ready. Not because I had all the answers, but because I trusted myself to figure them out. I've always said the best bet I'll ever make is on myself. When no one else does – I bet on me.

That confidence wasn't handed to me. I built it. I built it growing up poor. I built it watching my parents overcome addiction and keep our little family together when everything said we should fall apart. I built it when I started working for money at 13 years old.

My mom used to say, "The best fruit is out on the skinny branches." She was right. The skinny branches are risky. They bend. They might break. But they're where the good stuff lives. And if you want the good stuff, you've got to be willing to climb out there.

When I heard Tim Kight speak in 2018 about "The Edge," I felt like he was describing my life. Every major breakthrough I've had started right there, just past what I thought I was capable of. That's where skill is built. That's where champions are made. That's where the decision happens. You have a choice to retreat to safety, or step forward into growth and the best version of you.

Building skill is a mindset. It requires vigilance and discipline. It's not something you're born with. It's something you commit to. It's about showing up with curiosity, staying in the game through discomfort, and choosing every day to be a little better than you were the day before.

At Focus 3, we define the best version of you as better today than you were yesterday, and better tomorrow than you are today.

So when you hit "The Edge" – and you will – don't pull back. Don't regress back to where it feels safe and comfortable. Lean in. Be relentless. Embrace the discomfort. Use the feedback. Push past the fear. Let yourself be coached. Because

"The Edge" is not the end. It's the beginning of something even greater.

Focus 3 at Work

When you hit *an edge*, your life starts calling. Sometimes it's a whisper, and other times it can be a much louder voice from inside.

You can feel it in your bones. You know something has to shift, and you feel like you're going to crawl out of your skin if you don't act.

At Focus 3, we call those "edge moments." The times in life where you're being invited, sometimes shoved, into a better version of yourself. They usually fall into five buckets:

- Build skill.
- Get better at an existing skill.
- Change something.
- Start something.
- Stop something.

And when that edge shows up, it's almost always personal before it's professional.

We've had people tell us:

"I need to be a better listener."

"I need to start focusing on my health."

" I need to eat healthier."

"I need to stop drinking."

"I need to start showing up for my spouse."

"I need to stop operating on auto-pilot and actually *be present* with my kids."

And we've heard story after story of what happens when they do.

These aren't just performance tweaks. They're life-saving, relationship-repairing, identity-reclaiming shifts. And while we're brought into companies to "make teams better," what we're really doing is helping people *be better* because better people build better teams and better organizations.

That's why, without fail, at the end of every workshop, someone walks up with their workbook clutched in hand, eyes a little misty, and says, "Heather, I get it now. I know the company brought you in for performance. But what I'm really taking home is a new way to show up for my family."

And I love that. Because it's not one or the other.

It's both.

It's the *toggle* between personal and professional.

You can't separate them. You bring your energy, your mindset, your habits – *you* – to both places.

Picture this:

You walk into the office, ready to tackle that one big project. You've ramped your energy up to zone in, laser-focused. Ten minutes later, someone's standing in your doorway needing something. You ramp down to deal with it. Then back up to your project. Then a call. Then a fire drill. Up, down. Up, down. All day long.

And then you get home from a long day and wonder, *Why am I so tired? as you simply melt into the couch.*

It's because your energy has been on a rollercoaster all day. Emotional sprints, mental pivots, gear-shifting constantly. That's real. And it takes a toll.

Which is why, at the end of a workshop, we tell people, "Don't take your leftovers home. You've poured a lot into this room today. You've been present. Engaged. Intentional. Don't walk into your house and give the people you love most what's left over. *They* deserve your best, too."

When interviewing and on-boarding new members of the Focus 3 Team, we always have them sit in on a local R Factor workshop. After one of our workshops, one of the consultants we were interviewing shared this story in a text message to me:

"Heather, I have to tell you what happened. I went home today and was a better dad."

His daughter is on the spectrum. She is beautiful, bright, and often needs a lot from him. In the past, he'd be the first to admit, the exhaustion and stress sometimes got the best of him. He wasn't very patient at times and would snap at her. Then he would withdraw with guilt.

But that night, something changed. He said, "I caught myself in the moment. I paused. I got my mind right. And I stepped up. I met her where she was. With love. With calm. With presence."

That's what it means to *live* the work.

To *practice* it at home – not just preach it in the boardroom.

It's what happens when you realize that the edge you're facing isn't about your performance review. It's about your integrity. Your connection. Your calling.

We have had feedback from R Factor workshop attendees who said they were ready to walk away from their marriage.

Ready to leave their job.

Ready to give up on themselves.

And then they spent one day in a workshop.

They sat with the questions.

They did the work.

They caught a new vision for who they could be.

And they chose differently.

Not perfectly. But *intentionally.*

I always say, "We are not *human doings.* We're human *beings.*"

But we forget that, don't we?

We get swept up in the checklist, the grind, the pace. And at the end of the day, we might've crossed off twenty items but still feel like we didn't actually *accomplish* anything that mattered.

That's why this work is so important.

Because it brings us back to *ourselves.*

Back to our relationships.

Back to what actually matters.

—∞—

Perhaps the most impactful element of *The R Factor®* is its ability to transcend workplace application and be helpful – in real time – in one's personal life. The number one piece of feedback shared with Focus 3 is some iteration of this statement: "Yes, this system will help me at work, but the first thing I plan to do with this information is take it home and share it with my spouse and kids. The principles I've learned will help me not just at work, but at home as well. And I know it will help my family too."

Case in point, below is an email excerpt from a elementary school teacher in a mid-sized Ohio school district. Nikki (her name has been changed) participated in an R Factor® workshop in the first quarter of 2022 and, unsolicited, provided the following feedback:

"Recently I learned The R Factor® *can help us become better people overall, but it has helped me even more than that.*

Tuesday morning, I suffered a complete mental breakdown. Years of emotional and mental abuse from my ex-husband and from my current boyfriend finally broke me. I tried going to school so I could be with my students, but I could not gather my composure to even greet them as they walked into our classroom. I went to the doctor and she took me off work for the rest of the week and recommended counseling. She also talked about making self-care a priority. I am a mommy to five children and love my students as if they were my own. School is my happy place. Focus 3 was something that I found very compelling, but wasn't sure how to start applying it to work and my personal life, until yesterday when I broke down.

This morning as I prayed and counted my blessings, Focus 3 was one. I realized that what I was recently taught may be my saving grace. My goal for the next 30 days would be to press the pause button. Not only to think about my response, but to not let the negativity of others invade my 20 Square Feet. I sat at my kitchen table this morning, fighting off severe anxiety and reminded myself that it was not allowed in my 20 Square Feet. Negative comments from others, including my boyfriend, were not allowed in my 20 Square Feet. His lack of accountability for being part of the cause of my breakdown was not entering my 20 Square Feet. Narcissistic comments from him, or my ex-husband, were not permitted in my 20 Square Feet. Because of Focus 3, I am beginning to heal. I am setting boundaries and trying to gain strength and rebuild my self-esteem because of the principles Focus 3 is built upon.

Yet again, just this morning, my daughter and I were subpoenaed to court for an accident she was involved in, but not at fault. My daughter was very upset, but I used the teachings of Focus 3 to help her calm down. It is powerful. In a difficult moment, it helped my child. It helped us.

Never, in a million years, did I think it would help me fight these battles that cause so much anxiety and depression in my everyday life. But it has. I keep telling myself 'this is my 20 Square Feet and negativity is not welcome.' Focus 3 has changed my life."

Clearly this is an extreme example, but the reality is that the Focus 3 team receives similar feedback on a weekly basis. Sometimes in response to bigger events, sometimes smaller ones. The powerful framework of Event + Response =

Outcome is easily remembered, applied and shared. Only a system that is clear, simple and actionable is taken home from the workshop, webinar or keynote and shared with loved ones and friends.

Twenty-one months after Nikki's original email, upon following through she shared these comments:

"I must say that life is so good! You know, I never thought that incorporating The R Factor® *into my life would be such a game changer. In some of the hardest trials, it has really made things easier and more clear. And in the best times, I understand and appreciate more of how I was able to get into such a great place.*

Focus 3 came into my life at such a pivotal time where I needed to get ahold of myself and gain control of all of the events that were going on. The teachings have truly changed my life. I have become so much stronger mentally, which has led me to do things I didn't think I could. The strength that I have now is something I have never had. Knowing that I can own my mistakes and become better is something that is very powerful and really life changing. It's been a process. I really had to make E + R = O a priority and have done so, with amazing results."

—∞—

A Texas woman echoed the boundary-setting benefits of 20 Square Feet. She went on to talk about what she's learned in this way: *"The R Factor® solves problems. Period. That is why people want to share it with others. When the system is utilized, it helps immediately. But it is something that must be practiced over time."*

And when one is committed to those focused reps and doing the work, *The R Factor®* moves the needle in personal relationships as well as professional interactions. People are people and relational rules apply in every scenario, whether at home, at work, or elsewhere.

So what's your edge?

As we close out workshops, we ask every person. "What's the edge you're facing right now? What's the thing your life is asking you to start? To stop? To step up into?"

We don't ask that for dramatic effect. We ask because we *know* –

If you get better at home, you'll be better at work.

And if you grow at work, it spills over into home.

Great organizations aren't just built on performance. They're built on *people.*

People who are willing to grow *on purpose.*

And that includes you.

So wherever you're reading this from – whatever room, whatever season – you don't have to fix everything today. But you *can* do one thing:

Identify your edge.

Press pause.

Get your mind right.

Step up.

Because *you* at your best… changes everything, and it's what's best for those around you as well.

The Power of One

I've always said success only takes one. One person. One voice. One moment of belief spoken into your life with no agenda, no performance, no "what's in it for me" energy. Just someone who sees you...*really* sees you.

It's amazing how powerful that can be, especially when it comes from someone you trust. Someone who knows your story, your heart, your mess and chooses to speak life into you anyway. That kind of belief, even whispered, can change everything.

And yet, how many of us brush off our own brilliance? How many ideas have died in people's heads before they ever made it to paper or plan? I'm sure you've experienced it. It's that moment when there is a flicker of intuition, when your gut says, "This could be something," and your brain immediately slams it down with, "That's stupid. No one will care."

I think about that often. I think about all the lost ideas, the unrealized dreams, the people who never stepped out because no one looked them in the eye and said, "Yes, you can."

The only difference between people who live their dreams and those who don't isn't talent or luck. It's belief. And I don't mean just self-belief – I mean having someone else believe in you until you can believe in yourself.

Success, for me, isn't just about what you achieve. I tell the team all the time, it's like a chair with four legs. And if one leg's missing, the whole thing wobbles. The legs are spiritual, mental, physical, and financial…in that order.

Let me say that again. First, spiritual. You need a foundation that roots you. Hope. Faith. Meaning. Then mental. If your thoughts are all over the place, if you're spiraling in doubt or fear, it doesn't matter what else you have. Next is physical. My husband always says, "If you don't take care of your body, where are you going to live?" And he's right. You don't have to be an athlete, but you do need the strength, balance, and energy to move through life. Last is financial. If the first three are in place, the money has a way of following.

But if even one of those is broken, everything starts to fall apart. You can be a millionaire, but if your spirit is empty or your mind is chaotic or your body is failing, what good is the money?

That's why I come back to that one person. That one person who says, "I see you." That's what people are desperate for. Not more advice. Not more perfection. Just to be seen and known and loved exactly as they are.

So many of the struggles we're facing – anxiety, depression, loneliness – come back to that one thing. People don't feel seen.

I remember a friend asking me, "When you travel, do you get takeout and just eat alone in your room?"

I laughed. "What are you talking about? No, I go eat. If there's a restaurant in the hotel, I sit down and order what I want."

She looked at me like I had just confessed to committing a crime.

"You just sit there? By yourself?"

"Yes," I said. "I'm my own best company."

And I meant it.

I like what I think about. I enjoy my own company. I don't feel guilty about what I order. I might have an extra glass of wine. No one's there to judge me but me, and I don't judge me. I'm good with me.

It was Bob Proctor who said, "If *you* don't love *you*, who will?" And that stuck with me. I love me. Not in a performative, plaster-on-a-quote kind of way. In a real way. I've made peace with who I am and who I'm not.

And I think more women need that kind of peace.

For just a moment, let me address our female readers because somewhere along the line, we were taught that self-love is vanity. That confidence is arrogance. That celebrating ourselves is somehow selfish or inappropriate.

But here's the truth – there's nothing more powerful than a woman who likes herself. Not just tolerates herself, not just survives her days, but genuinely enjoys who she is, and walks through life with a healthy sense of self and confidence.

That's the root of so much healing. And I'll say it again… it all starts with one. One person. One belief. One voice that tells you the truth about who you are, even when you can't see it for yourself. That voice can be your own!

You are seen. You're not broken. You're not behind. You're not too late. You are already enough, and you're allowed to like yourself.

In fact, you're meant to.

Ready to Do the Work?

So now…it's time to go do the work.

Not in the hustle-harder, no pain/no gain, burn-yourself-out kind of way.

But in the real way. It's time to create change that matters.

What does "the work" mean for you?

For some, it's pressing pause before reacting.

For others, it's stopping something that's been holding you back.

Maybe it's stepping up in your marriage. Or being more present with your kids.

Maybe it's finally having that hard conversation.

Or taking a breath before walking into the office each day, reminding yourself who you want to be.

Whatever it is, I want to invite you into something intentional. Something real.

It's what we call a 30-Day Challenge.

Based on what you've read or maybe experienced in a Focus 3 workshop, take one thing – just one – and commit to it for 30 days.

Don't overthink it. Don't wait for the perfect timing.

Decide what skill you want to build or improve. Why is that skill important to you right now? What's your game plan?

And because we believe in walking alongside people, not just cheering from the sidelines, we're creating a simple way to stay connected.

You'll find a QR code in this book that links directly to our Focus 3 team. Tap it, and a short form will pop up with just one question:

What's your 30-Day Challenge?

From there, you'll have the option to hear from someone on our team. No pressure. Just real people, supporting real growth, with real accountability.

Because you weren't made to do this alone. And you don't have to.

So go ahead. Take the step.

Say yes to doing the work.

And if you're ready, let us walk with you.

Continuing on the Journey

Thank you for spending time with this book and walking alongside me through the lessons of The R Factor. Writing this wasn't something I ever imagined doing, but life is full of edges, and I'm grateful for the opportunity to step into this one.

My hope is that these stories and principles have resonated with you. That you not only see how The R Factor has shaped my journey, but that it's given you a powerful framework to shape your own. The real impact of this work is what happens when you apply it – with intention, with discipline, and with purpose – in your everyday life.

One of the questions we hear most often after people experience The R Factor is:

"What's next?"

If you're asking that question, I'm excited for you. Because the journey doesn't end here. In fact, this is just the beginning.

Here are four great ways you can go deeper:

Focus 3+ (On-Demand Virtual Training)

Access The R Factor anytime, anywhere. Our Focus 3+ platform includes our full R Factor training, plus an expanding library of video lessons and leadership resources to help you build skill and stay consistent.

Join today at Focus3.com/plus

Public Workshops

There's nothing quite like being in the room. Join our team at one of our live public workshops, where we teach The R Factor in person and connect you with others on the same journey. You'll leave energized, equipped, and ready to lead with clarity and discipline.

See upcoming events at Focus3.com/events

The 30-Day Challenge

Start strong. If you're ready to build the habit of discipline-driven behavior, our guided 30-Day Challenge is a great next step. It's simple, practical, and powerful – and it's designed to help you put The R Factor principles into motion in your daily life.

Take the challenge at Focus3.com/30

The R Factor Around the Dinner Table

This framework can also be integrated into everyday family life. Designed for parents, it shows how simple moments like meals and car rides can become opportunities to teach children how to pause, think, and choose their response. The program offers practical tools to improve communication, strengthen relationships, and help kids build habits that support personal responsibility and stronger decision-making at home.

See more at Focus3.com

Final Thoughts

At the beginning of this book I shared the story of my huge resistance to writing the book and how I didn't think I even had a book.

Not only that, when I met with Kelli Watson at Scriptor Publishing I did my very best to convince her that I didn't have a book and worked diligently to position our conversation in such a way that I was sure she would agree with me! I couldn't have been more wrong!

It's not only that I was wrong, it was Kelli's compelling argument that not only did I have a book, I had a story to share.

Throughout my life as you have read I have had several highly influential people and moments that have continually directed my next steps.

I have often heard and repeated that all it takes is that ONE person who can make such a dramatic impact in and on your life.

I wanted to take this opportunity to thank Kelli, Greg, and the entire Scriptor Publishing Team for guiding me through this process and showing me that I did have a book, that I did have a story to share and that they could guide me through the process.

I also want to encourage you to listen to that small, still voice that speaks to YOU as you stare up at the ceiling in the wee hours of the morning and calls you to The Edge of what's next and calls you to fulfill your dreams.

Because that ONE person could actually be YOU calling YOU to the best version of self.

Your edge is calling. Are you ready, and willing, to answer?

www.ingramcontent.com/pod-product-compliance
Lightning Source LLC
LaVergne TN
LVHW010839120826
845149LV00017B/3315